THE LIVES OF WOLVES

Wolves Discovery Library

Lynn M. Stone

The Rourke Book Company, Inc.
Vero Beach, Florida 32964

PHOTO CREDITS
© Lynn M. Stone: cover, title page, p.4, 6, 8, 10, 12,
13, 14, 16, 19.
© L. David Mech: p.21

EDITORIAL SERVICES
Penworthy Learning Systems

Library of Congress Cataloging-in-Publication Data

Stone, Lynn M.
    The lives of wolves / Lynn Stone.
        p. cm. — (Wolves discovery library)
    Summary: Describes wolves, including their appearance, behavior, and
habitat.
    ISBN 1-55916-239-2
    1. Wolves—Juvenile literature. [1. Wolves.] I. Title.

QL737.C22 S763 2000
599.773—dc21
                                                00-020870

Printed in the USA

CONTENTS

WHAT IS A WOLF?

A big dog is not quite the same as a wolf. But it's close. After all, a wolf is just a big, wild dog.

Scientists call members of the dog family **canids**. The wild canids include wolves, jackals, foxes, coyotes, **dholes**, and several kinds of wild dogs. Canids are one of the groups of meat-eating mammals. Mammals are animals that raise their babies on milk. Land mammals have four legs and fur or hair.

Wolves in Canada feast on a white-tailed deer. Working in packs, wolves regularly kill animals bigger than themselves.

WHAT WOLVES LOOK LIKE

Wolves are the largest wild canids. Wolves in North America usually weigh between 80 and 120 pounds (36–55 kg). The largest wolf reported weighed 175 pounds (80 kg). It was a male wolf in Alaska.

Wolves in North America stand 26 to 32 inches (66–82 cm) tall at their shoulders. They measure from about 54 to 78 inches (138–200 cm) in length. Length is measured from the tip of a wolf's nose to the tip of its tail. A wolf's tail is from 13 to 20 inches (33–51 cm) long.

Wolves have coats of many colors. The wolf's fur is at its finest during the winter, when warmth is important.

A wolf has a long, fairly sharp nose and long, thick fur, especially in winter. A wolf's fur may be white, gray, or even black.

Most wolves' coats are a mixture of white, gray, and brown. Wolves in North America are often called "gray" wolves.

Wolves have bushy tails, upright ears, and claws on their toes. Canid claws are different from those of cats, or felines. Canid claws are blunt, not sharp like cat claws. Cat claws move in and out of a cat's paws. Canid claws are set in place.

The wolf has a long, slender muzzle, rich fur, and erect ears. A snarl can instantly erase the wolf's kindly look.

LIVING IN NATURE

Like other canids, wolves were made to run and hunt. Wolves have long legs to help them run fast. Long legs also help wolves move through deep snow.

The wolf has long, sharp front teeth called **fangs**. Fangs help a wolf bite and tear into the animals it hunts. As a **predator**, or hunter, the wolf makes its living by killing other animals, its **prey**. Wolves hunt together in family groups called **packs**. Each pack has from 3 to 30 wolves. An average pack has 5 to 7 wolves. Sometimes, however, a wolf lives alone.

The wolf is wrapped in a long, silky coat of fur.
If the falling snow becomes a nuisance, the
wolf will shake it off.

More wolves live in the woodlands of Minnesota than in any other of the lower 48 states.

*These two wolves don't seem at all moved by the pack
leader's howling solo.*

Each wild animal has a role, or job, in nature. The wolf's role is to kill and eat large mammals, such as deer or moose. By hunting together, wolves can kill animals much bigger than themselves.

Predators must rely on their senses. The wolf, like the tame dog, has a super sense of smell. When the wind blows toward a wolf, it can smell prey up to one and one-half miles (2.4 km) away. The wolf has good eyesight and hearing, too. Wolves can hear other wolves howling several miles away.

Wolves make a kill together. (Scientists call it "cooperative hunting.") Then the pack feeds together. Packs usually have five to seven members.

WHERE WOLVES LIVE

Long ago, wolves lived in more places than any mammal except humans. Wolves no longer live in so many places. People have killed thousands of wolves and their prey. But wolves still live in parts of North America, Europe, Asia, and North Africa.

Canada probably has more wolves than any other country. About 50,000 wolves live throughout Canada, from British Columbia eastward into Quebec, Ontario, and Labrador. Wolves even live in the Far North on the cold islands of the Arctic Ocean.

Wolves live in some of the most rugged and beautiful places on earth. This is Denali National Park, Alaska, the best place to see wild wolves.

The United States has perhaps 10,000 wolves. Most of them live in Alaska. Most of the others live in states bordering Canada. Minnesota may have as many as 2,000 wolves. Michigan and Wisconsin have perhaps 100 wolves each. Several dozen wolves live in Montana and Wyoming. A few wolves live in Idaho, Washington, North Dakota and New Mexico. North Carolina has a small population of red wolves.

The special kind of area in which a wild plant or animal lives is its **habitat**. Wolves live in many habitats. Wolves can live in any natural habitat in the northern half of the world except deserts or tropical forests.

Wolves from neighboring Canada slipped into Glacier National Park, Montana, and began new packs there in the 1990s.

Wolves in the Arctic live on open, treeless plains called **tundra**. Other wolves live in forests. Some live in areas with a mix of forests and open land.

Wolves used to be common on the grassy prairies of the American West. These "buffalo wolves" followed buffalo (bison) herds.

The buffalo wolves, also called plains wolves, were killed off by white settlers in the 19th and early 20th centuries. Today, however, wolves once again prowl American grasslands in Yellowstone National Park.

Wolves live in a variety of habitats. These Arctic wolf pups live on the tundra of northern Canada.

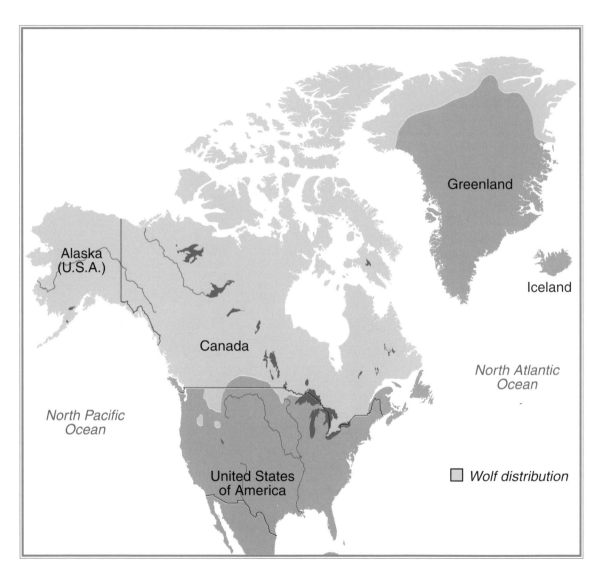

Alaska
(U.S.A.)

Canada

Greenland

Iceland

North Atlantic
Ocean

North Pacific
Ocean

United States
of America

☐ *Wolf distribution*

GLOSSARY

canid (KAY nid) – any of the wild or domestic dogs; a canine

dhole (DOL) – a wild dog of India

fang (FANG) – long, sharp front tooth

habitat (HAB eh tat) – the special kind of place in which an animal lives, such as evergreen forest

pack (PAK) – a group of wolves that lives and hunts together in helpful ways

predator (PRED uh ter) – an animal that hunts and kills other animals for food

prey (PRAY) – an animal that is hunted for food by another animal

tundra (TUI IN druh) – the cold, treeless land of the Arctic; the cover of small plants and lichens that carpets the land of the Arctic region

FURTHER INFORMATION

Find out more about wolves with these helpful books and websites:

International Wolf Center on line at www.wolf.org

Lawrence, R.D. **Wolves**. Sierra Club, 1990

Patent, Dorothy Hinshaw. **Gray Wolf Red Wolf**. Clarion, 1990

Swinburne, Stephen. **Once a Wolf**. Houghton Mifflin, 1999

INDEX